www.gardenpublishingco.com

Spirit of Truth

The Garden Training Center, Inc.
An Apostolic School of Ministry

Copyright ©2020 by The Garden Training Center, Inc.
Published by Garden Publishing Company LLC
For more information, please visit gardenpublishingco.com

All rights reserved. No parts of this publication may be reproduced, stored in a retrieval system, or transmitted in any form or by any means, electronic, mechanical, photocopying, recording, or otherwise, without the prior written permission of the copyright owner.

This book is sold subject to the condition that it shall not, by way of trade or otherwise, be lent, resold, hired out, or otherwise circulated without the publisher's prior consent in any form of binding or cover other than that in which it is published and without a similar condition including this condition being imposed on the subsequent purchaser. Under no circumstances may any part of this book be photocopied for resale.

Scripture taken from the New King James Version of the Bible ©. Used by Permission, all rights reserved.

ISBN 978-1-7355464-2-1
Cover design by Garden Publishing Co./Whitney Whitt
Interior design by Garden Publishing Co.

Printed in the United States of America.

Acknowledgments

Holy Spirit is the inspiration for the content of this book, however someone put words to it. This book was written by Danetta Ferguson and Brandy Helton.

This book is one of a series of books written and distributed by The Apostolic School of Ministry from The Garden Training Center, Inc. The series arises from the foundational teachings of the school of ministry, founded by Brandy Helton. Brandy wrote several sections that are included in each book such as "God's Love" and the prayers included at the end of each book.

Many thanks to the team of writers of the series for their collaboration to make the series available to the public. The writers are: Lauren Caldwell, Jessica Doggett, Danetta Ferguson, Elisa Griffith, Nancy Hadley, Robin Harmon, Brandy Helton, Grant Hill, and Kevin McSpadden. Each have sought Holy Spirit for the words He wants to speak through them. The result is a mixture of personalities and communication strategies that convey the total message in a beautiful, diverse way.

A special thanks goes to Nancy Hadley, and Chelsey Butcher with Garden Publishing Co., for their preparation and fine tuning of the text.

Encouragement and Prayer for the Reader

Beloved of God, these teachings are written to reveal Jesus Christ and His heart of love for all who call upon His name to save them.

God has sent His only begotten Son, Jesus Christ, to save all who would believe in Him and His Word.

God desires to reveal Himself and to give us His divine nature in Christ Jesus our Lord through the power of His Holy Spirit.

God is Jealous. He wants us to encounter His presence daily and walk with Him in glory – intimate communion - today, while it is called today, and forever.

It is my prayer that this teaching would so impact the readers that all would come to know and believe JESUS, the King of Kings and Lord of Lords, our Great God and Savior, and receive the PERFECT LOVE He has for us all as we grow up into Him and mature as true sons and daughters of God.

May you grow in faith and knowledge of your God and Savior and come to know the love that He has for you. I pray for you the Apostle Paul's prayer for spiritual growth:

Ephesians 3:14-21 The Living Bible (TLB)
"14-15 When I think of the wisdom and scope of his plan, I fall down on my knees and pray to the Father of all the great family of God—some of them already in heaven and some down here on earth— 16 that out of his glorious, unlimited resources he will give you the mighty inner strengthening of his Holy Spirit. 17 And I pray that Christ will be more and more at home in your hearts, living within you as you trust in him. May your roots go down deep into the soil of God's marvelous love; 18-19 and may you be able to feel and understand, as all God's children should, how long, how wide, how deep, and how high his love really is; and to experience this love for yourselves, though it is so great that you will never see the end of it or fully know or understand it. And so at last you will be filled up with God himself.
20 Now glory be to God, who by his mighty power at work within us is able to do far more than we would ever dare to ask or even dream of—infinitely beyond our highest prayers, desires, thoughts, or hopes. 21 May he be given glory forever and ever through endless ages because of his master plan of salvation for the Church through Jesus Christ."

In Christ our Lord,
Brandy Helton
A child of God

God's Love

God's love is good news! Don't believe the lie that God is distant, unapproachable, and angry!

God is love. He is the only true, eternal God. He is perfect and holy, and He is truth. God is One. He has revealed Himself in three distinct, individual, equal persons: God the Father, God the Son – Jesus, and God the Holy Spirit.

The Bible tells the story of God's perfect love. In that love, God created the first family to live on the earth with Him. Through their deep intimate relationship with the Father, Adam and Eve were meant to fulfill all that was in God's heart on Earth just like it is in Heaven, for God's glory and purposes. Adam and Eve were chosen to walk with God, clothed in His glory presence and were perfect, as He is perfect, and they lived in His beautiful garden, the secret place called Eden. He gave them His breath, life and power to have dominion over all He created and wanted them to reproduce that LIFE replenishing the earth with it, until all the earth is filled with His glory.

Genesis 1:26-28
"26 Then God said, 'Let Us make man in Our

image, according to Our likeness; let them have dominion over the fish of the sea, over the birds of the air, and over the cattle, over all the earth and over every creeping thing that creeps on the earth.' 27 So God created man in His own image; in the image of God He created him; male and female He created them. 28 Then God blessed them, and God said to them, 'Be fruitful and multiply; fill the earth and subdue it; have dominion over the fish of the sea, over the birds of the air, and over every living thing that moves on the earth.'"

God created His children in His likeness. He made them spirit beings, with a soul – mind, will and emotions – and placed them in a physical body. He gave His children the choice to love Him and to walk with Him in obedience to His every word. He gave the first family the power to overcome any temptation offered to them through God's adversary, the devil, who had rebelled against the Most High God in Heaven's glory and was cast down to the earth. The devil, Satan, brought great darkness and chaos prior to Adam and Eve's existence.

Adam and Eve were deceived into thinking that God was not perfect in love as Satan, the adversary, tempted them to believe that God would not keep His Word to them. Through their own will, Adam and Eve disobeyed the Father by eating from a tree that had the power to open their eyes to both good and evil. Through their choice of disobedience, they willfully gave their inheritance and authority over to the devil and his kingdom. Sin entered mankind, which produced death, eternal separation from a Holy God. Adam and Eve were banished from the dwelling and intimacy of perfection in the garden and were sent into the world as a fallen creation.

Father God knew He had to come Himself and save His family, and in His wisdom, He chose to send His Son, Jesus Christ into the world to save us and restore fallen mankind back to relationship with Him. Through His Son, He destroyed all the works of the devil and the curse of death. Hebrews 9:22 says, *"And according to the law almost all things are purified with blood, and without shedding of blood there is no remission."* Remission means to cancel the penalty, so according to the law there must be shedding of blood to cancel the penalty for sin. The Father cancelled the penalty for the sins of His children through the shedding of the blood of His innocent, holy Son Jesus, who was the Sent One, called and chosen to die for all, so all could live.

John 3:16-21
"16 For God so loved the world that He gave His only begotten Son, that whoever believes in Him should not perish but have everlasting life. 17 For God did not send His Son into the world to condemn the world, but that the world through Him might be saved. 18 'He who believes in Him is not condemned; but he who does not believe is condemned already, because he has not believed in the name of the only begotten Son of God. 19 And this is the condemnation, that the light has come into the world, and men loved darkness rather than light, because their deeds were evil. 20 For everyone practicing evil hates the light and does not come to the light, lest his deeds should be exposed. 21 But he who does the truth comes to the light, that his deeds may

be clearly seen, that they have been done in God."'

Jesus was conceived by God's Holy Spirit in the womb of a young virgin named Mary. He appeared as the second Adam, in the flesh, with the choice to walk in perfect love and obedience, full of God's Spirit, as a man to do the will of His Father.

Jesus grew up as any male child did in the flesh but He had divine fellowship with His Father and Holy Spirit. At the appointed time, He was revealed as being sent from God to save. Jesus went around doing good and healed all who were oppressed by the devil spiritually and physically. He revealed His Father's heart and perfect love to all who believed through His teachings, grace and miraculous power.

Salvation means eternal life, healing, deliverance, protection, peace, wholeness, and forgiveness. Salvation came to all men through the cross, where the Son of God, the perfect One, was slaughtered as a lamb, bearing all sin for all times from a fallen people. Jesus bore the wrath of God against the darkness that separated God's family from Him. Jesus was punished for our sin and died to cleanse us from the guilt, shame and condemnation sin produces. Sin separates. Love restores.

Jesus was crucified, dead and buried, spending three days and nights in the depths of Hades, the realm of the dead fallen race. Jesus took back the keys of death and hell from that old serpent the devil, Satan, and therefore, all authority was restored back to Jesus.

Great Holy Spirit breathed LIFE into Jesus and raised Him from the dead. He appeared to His disciples, those who followed Him and obeyed His teachings. He showed them that He conquered sin, death and the grave and now, had the keys of hell and death, and would give ETERNAL LIFE to ALL who chose to believe in Him. King Jesus ascended back to the Father of glory where He ever lives to make intercession for us all, and He is coming again to the earth in power to establish His Father's Kingdom on Earth.

Jesus Christ is the head and Lord over His church, those who have made Him Lord and Savior, by believing He is the Son of the Living God and God in the flesh, who finished the work the Father gave Him to do. He not only died for our sins to save and heal us, He chose to give His authority to those He called and chose to follow Him as His disciples, His family.

Jesus has commissioned His followers to do the same works that He did while He lived on the earth.

John 14:12-14
"12 Most assuredly, I say to you, he who believes in Me, the works that I do he will do also; and greater works than these he will do, because I go to My Father. 13 And whatever you ask in My name, that I will do, that the Father may be glorified in the Son. 14 If you ask anything in My name, I will do it."

God loves us and desires that none should perish. He desires for His family to be with Him where He is. These books are written to inspire all who read them and to reveal the heart of God the Father, Jesus Christ the Son, and Holy Spirit in order that we might RECEIVE THE LOVE HE HAS FOR US and be CHANGED INTO HIS VERY LIKENESS. God desires to dwell with His family forever and ever just as He did in the beginning. How glorious it is to live in His presence and dominion, beholding His goodness, forever and ever, amen.

The book of Revelation describes the time that is coming when all things are made new according to God's heart of love:

Revelation 21:1-7
"1 Now I saw a new heaven and a new earth, for the first heaven and the first earth had passed away. Also, there was no more sea. 2 Then I, John, saw the holy city, New Jerusalem, coming down out of heaven from God, prepared as a bride adorned for her husband. 3 And I heard a loud voice from heaven saying, 'Behold, the tabernacle of God is with men, and He will dwell with them, and they shall be His people. God Himself will be with them and be their God. 4 And God will wipe away every tear from their eyes; there shall be no more death, nor sorrow, nor crying. There shall be no more pain, for the former things have passed away.' 5 Then He who sat on the throne said, 'Behold, I make all things new.' And He said to me, 'Write, for these words are true and faithful.' 6 And He said to me, 'It is done! I am the Alpha and the Omega, the Beginning and the End. I will give of the fountain of the water of life freely to him who thirsts. 7 He who overcomes shall inherit all things, and I will be his God and he shall be

My son.'"

To understand what is presented in the Bible, you must start by understanding God's love. The good news is that God loves you!

The Heart of It

The purpose of this teaching is to bring great honor to Holy Spirit and to reveal His glorious passion and identity as The Spirit of Truth. All believers of Jesus Christ who have made Jesus their personal Lord and Savior have Holy Spirit living inside of them. He leads, protects, comforts, directs, teaches and empowers the children of God. He empowers all believers to be true witnesses of the resurrected Christ. Holy Spirit is truth; therefore, His very essence will deliver the children of God from deception and lies that war against the Word of God. Through this teaching, the believer will encounter the ways of Holy Spirit and learn the importance of knowing Him intimately as Lord, as He prepares each person for King Jesus and His eternal destiny.

Spirit of Truth

What does the Christian really believe?

The Word of God – The Bible

Jesus said in John 17:17, *'Thy word is truth.'* The Bible is the inspired, infallible Word of God. Both Old and New Testaments are fully inspired by the Holy Spirit, without error and an infallible guide in matters pertaining to life and godliness. It reveals God's complete will for the salvation of mankind. His Word is trustworthy, and the supreme authority in all points of doctrine, life and godliness.

II Timothy 3:16
"*16 All Scripture is given by inspiration of God, and is profitable for doctrine, for reproof, for correction, for instruction in righteousness.*"

II Peter 1:20-21
"*20 knowing this first, that no prophecy of Scripture is of any private interpretation, 21 for prophecy never came by the will of man, but holy men of God spoke as they were moved by the Holy Spirit.*"

Hebrews 4:12-13
"12 For the word of God is living and powerful, and sharper than any two-edged sword, piercing even to the division of soul and spirit, and of joints and marrow, and is a discerner of the thoughts and intents of the heart. 13 And there is no creature hidden from His sight, but all things are naked and open to the eyes of Him to whom we must give account."

The Godhead

There is only one true, eternal God. He is love, perfect, holy, and truth. God is One. He has revealed Himself in three distinct, individual, equal persons: God the Father, God the Son – Jesus Christ (The Word that became flesh), and God the Holy Spirit.

I John 5:7
"7 For there are three that bear witness in heaven: the Father, the Word, and the Holy Spirit; and these three are one."

John 1:1-4
"1 In the beginning was the Word, and the Word was with God, and the Word was God. 2 He was in the beginning with God. 3 All things were made through Him, and without Him nothing was made that was made. 4 In Him was life, and the life was the light of men."

John 1:14
"14 And the Word became flesh and dwelt among us, and we beheld His glory, the glory as of the only begotten of the Father, full of grace and truth."

John 1:18
"18 No one has seen God at any time. The only begotten Son, who is in the bosom of the Father, He has declared Him."

John 1:29
"29 The next day John saw Jesus coming toward him, and said, 'Behold! The Lamb of God who takes away the sin of the world!'"

John 1:32-34
"32 And John bore witness, saying, 'I saw the Spirit descending from heaven like a dove, and He remained upon Him. 33 I did not know Him, but He who sent me to baptize with water said to me, "Upon whom you see the Spirit descending, and remaining on Him, this is He who baptizes with the Holy Spirit." 34 And I have seen and testified that this is the Son of God."

Luke 3:21-22
"21 When all the people were baptized, it came to pass that Jesus also was baptized; and while He prayed, the heaven was opened. 22 And the Holy Spirit descended in bodily form like a dove upon Him, and a voice came from heaven which said, 'You are My beloved Son; in You I am well pleased."

Matthew 28:18-19
"18 And Jesus came and spoke to them, saying, 'All authority has been given to Me in heaven and on earth. 19 Go therefore and make disciples of all the nations, baptizing them in the name of the Father and of the Son and of the Holy Spirit.'"

God the Father is the Creator and Author of All Life.

Genesis 1:1-2
"1 In the beginning God created the heavens and the earth. 2 The earth was without form, and void; and darkness was on the face of the deep. And the Spirit of God was hovering over the face of the waters."

Exodus 3:13-14
"13 Then Moses said to God, 'Indeed, when I come to the children of Israel and say to them, "The God of your fathers has sent me to you," and they say to me, "What is His name?" what shall I say to them?' 14 And God said to Moses, 'I AM WHO I AM.' And He said, 'Thus you shall say to the children of Israel, "I AM has sent me to you."'"

Isaiah 51:13
"13 And you forget the Lord your Maker, Who stretched out the heavens and laid the foundations of the earth."

Matthew 6:9-10
"9 In this manner, therefore, pray: Our Father in heaven, Hallowed be Your name. 10 Your kingdom come. Your will be done on earth as it is in heaven."

I John 4:12-16
"12 No one has seen God at any time. If we love one another, God abides in us, and His love has been perfected in us. 13 By this we know that we abide in Him, and He in us, because He has

given us of His Spirit. 14 And we have seen and testify that the Father has sent the Son as Savior of the world. 15 Whoever confesses that Jesus is the Son of God, God abides in him, and he in God. 16 And we have known and believed the love that God has for us. God is love, and he who abides in love abides in God, and God in him."

Matthew 5:48
"48 Therefore you shall be perfect, just as your Father in heaven is perfect."

God the Son, Jesus Christ, Creator of all things with the Father, was manifest in the flesh, fully God, yet fully man, conceived by the Holy Spirit, born of the virgin Mary, anointed and empowered by the Holy Spirit to bring God's Kingdom to Earth. He was crucified, dead, and buried, resurrected bodily on the third day according to the Scriptures, and appeared to His disciples. He ascended to Heaven, where He sits at the right hand of God the Father, and continually intercedes for His people. Jesus will return for His pure, spotless, glorious church and execute judgment upon the wicked.

John 3:16
"16 For God so loved the world that He gave His only begotten Son, that whoever believes in Him should not perish but have everlasting life."

Matthew 1:23
"23 'Behold, the virgin shall be with child, and bear a Son, and they shall call His name Immanuel,' which is translated, 'God with us.'"

John 5:18

"*18 Therefore the Jews sought all the more to kill Him (Jesus), because He not only broke the Sabbath, but also said that God was His Father, making Himself equal with God.*"

Philippians 2:5-11

"*5...Christ Jesus, 6 who, being in the form of God, did not consider it robbery to be equal with God, 7 but made Himself of no reputation, taking the form of a bondservant, and coming in the likeness of men. 8 And being found in appearance as a man, He humbled Himself and became obedient to the point of death, even the death of the cross. 9 Therefore God also has highly exalted Him and given Him the name which is above every name, 10 that at the name of Jesus every knee should bow, of those in heaven, and of those on earth, and of those under the earth, 11 and that every tongue should confess that Jesus Christ is Lord, to the glory of God the Father.*"

Colossians 1:15-20

"*15 He (Jesus) is the image of the invisible God, the firstborn over all creation. 16 For by Him all things were created that are in heaven and that are on earth, visible and invisible, whether thrones or dominions or principalities or powers. All things were created through Him and for Him. 17 And He is before all things, and in Him all things consist. 18 And He is the head of the body, the church, who is the beginning, the firstborn from the dead, that in all things He may have the preeminence. 19 For it pleased the Father that in Him all the fullness should dwell, 20 and by Him to reconcile all things to*

Himself, by Him, whether things on earth or things in heaven, having made peace through the blood of His cross."

I Corinthians 15:3-5
"3 ...Christ died for our sins according to the Scriptures, 4 and that He was buried, and that He rose again the third day according to the Scriptures, 5 and that He was seen by Cephas, then by the twelve."

Acts 1:9-11
"9 Now when He (Jesus) had spoken these things, while they watched, He was taken up, and a cloud received Him out of their sight. 10 And while they looked steadfastly toward heaven as He went up, behold, two men stood by them in white apparel, 11 who also said, 'Men of Galilee, why do you stand gazing up into heaven? This same Jesus, who was taken up from you into heaven, will so come in like manner as you saw Him go into heaven.'"

Hebrews 1:1-4
"1 God, who at various times and in various ways spoke in time past to the fathers by the prophets, 2 has in these last days spoken to us by His Son, whom He has appointed heir of all things, through whom also He made the worlds; 3 who being the brightness of His glory and the express image of His person, and upholding all things by the word of His power, when He had by Himself purged our sins, sat down at the right hand of the Majesty on high, 4 having become so much better than the angels, as He has by inheritance obtained a more excellent name than they."

Acts 17:31
"31 because He (God) has appointed a day on which He will judge the world in righteousness by the Man whom He has ordained (Jesus). He (God) has given assurance of this to all by raising Him (Jesus) from the dead."

Ephesians 5:23-27
"23 For the husband is head of the wife, as also Christ is head of the church; and He is the Savior of the body. 24 Therefore, just as the church is subject to Christ, so let the wives be to their own husbands in everything. 25 Husbands, love your wives, just as Christ also loved the church and gave Himself for her, 26 that He might sanctify and cleanse her with the washing of water by the word, 27 that He might present her to Himself a glorious church, not having spot or wrinkle or any such thing, but that she should be holy and without blemish."

The Holy Spirit is the Spirit of Truth, Comforter, Promise of the Father and the One who reveals Christ and His work on the cross. He is the Spirit of Holiness that raised Christ Jesus from the dead. The Holy Spirit dwells within all believers, sanctifying believers and enabling them to live holy, supernatural lives.

John 14:16-17
"16 And I will ask the Father, and He will give you another Helper, that He may be with you forever; 17 that is the Spirit of Truth, whom the world cannot receive, because it does not behold Him or know Him, but you know Him because He abides with you, and will be in you."

John 15:26
"26 When the Helper comes, whom I will send to you from the Father, that is the Spirit of Truth, who proceeds from the Father, He will bear witness of Me."

John 16:13-15
"13 But when He, the Spirit of Truth comes, He will guide you into all truth; for He will not speak of His own initiative, but whatever He hears, He will speak and He will disclose what is to come. 14 And He shall glorify Me (Jesus); for He will take of Mine and shall disclose it to you. 15 All things that the Father has are Mine; therefore, I said that He shall take of Mine and disclose it you."

I John 4:6
"6 We (believers) are from God; he who knows God listens to us; he who is not from God does not listen to us. By this we know the spirit of truth and the spirit of error."

Ephesians 1:13
"13 In Him (Jesus) you also trusted, after you heard the word of truth, the gospel of your salvation; in whom also, having believed, you were sealed with the Holy Spirit of promise."

I Corinthians 3:17-18
"17 Now the Lord is the Spirit; and where the Spirit of the Lord is, there is liberty. 18 But we all, with unveiled face, beholding as in a mirror the glory of the Lord, are being transformed into the same image from glory to glory, just as by the Spirit of the Lord."

Acts 2:33
"33 Therefore being exalted to the right hand of God and having received from the Father the promise of the Holy Spirit, He (Jesus) poured out this (Holy Spirit) which you now see and hear."

The Holy Spirit was given to believers at Pentecost in such a powerful way that the event is described as an outpouring of the Holy Spirit. Holy Spirit is a gift from God to empower all believers as promised by the Lord Jesus Christ. The Holy Spirit gives gifts to believers for empowerment to be witnesses of Jesus Christ and His finished work on the cross and His glorious resurrection from the dead.

Matthew 3:11
"11 I (John the Baptist) indeed baptize you with water unto repentance, but He (Jesus) who is coming after me is mightier than I, whose sandals I am not worthy to carry. He will baptize you with the Holy Spirit and fire."

Acts 1:8
"8 But you shall receive power when the Holy Spirit has come upon you; and you shall be witnesses to Me (Jesus) in Jerusalem, and in all Judea and Samaria, and to the end of the earth."

Acts 2:1-4
"1 When the Day of Pentecost had fully come, they were all with one accord in one place. 2 And suddenly there came a sound from heaven, as of a rushing mighty wind, and it filled the

whole house where they were sitting. 3 Then there appeared to them divided tongues, as of fire, and one sat upon each of them. 4 And they were all filled with the Holy Spirit and began to speak with other tongues, as the Spirit gave them utterance."

Acts 2:38-39

"38 Then Peter said to them, 'Repent, and let every one of you be baptized in the name of Jesus Christ for the remission of sins; and you shall receive the gift of the Holy Spirit. 39 For the promise is to you and to your children, and to all who are afar off, as many as the Lord our God will call.'"

Mark 16:15-18

"15 Go into all the world and preach the gospel to every creature. 16 He who believes and is baptized will be saved; but he who does not believe will be condemned. 17 And these signs shall follow those who believe: In My (Jesus) name they will cast out demons; and they will speak with new tongues; 18 they will take up serpents; and if they drink anything deadly, it will by no means harm them; they will lay hands on the sick and they will recover."

The Lordship of Holy Spirit

We know that we are made in the image of God. God is a three part being (Father, Son and Holy Spirit). Because we are made in that image, we are a three part being, too. We are a spirit being, we have a soul (mind, will and emotion) and we live in our bodies. When we are born again, Holy Spirit comes to live in our spirit man to quicken it and bring it to life. At that moment, our spirit man is made perfect because God's very spirit is alive in us. However, our soul area and our bodies are not perfected at that very moment. As we surrender to His Lordship, our spirit man grows and grows and begins to change the areas of our mind, will, and emotion. It is a process called sanctification. Jesus used the term 'born again' to make it very clear to us that we are a new creation.

When a baby is newly born, he or she does baby things. Babies aren't in trouble because they can't crawl or walk within minutes of their birth. Why? They haven't reached that level of maturity yet. In the same way, when we are new believers, we are still immature and growing. Some sins will fall away immediately, and some are in process. Some things I did as a new believer, I didn't realize were sin until I reached a certain place of maturity and Holy Spirit convicted me of it. Once convicted, I was responsible to surrender that sin to the Father, repent and stop doing it. If I continue to sin after I know it is sin, that is lawlessness. This will continue until the day we see Jesus face to face because He is growing us up and refining us to be mature sons and daughters. It is a daily surrender. It is sometimes a minute by minute surrender...but there must be surrender.

We have seen in the Scriptures that God the Father is Lord; and we have seen where Jesus is Lord. Did you know that Holy Spirit is Lord, too? Just as we surrender to the Father and Son as Lord, we are to surrender to Holy Spirit as Lord. In fact, 2 Corinthians 3:17 says:

"17 Now the Lord is the Spirit; and where the

Spirit of the Lord is, there is liberty."

The Lord is the Spirit. Just as we saw that Jesus came to destroy the works of the devil, we can see in this passage that the Spirit destroys the works of the devil, too. He brings liberty. Liberty from what? He brings liberty from the evil one and his works against us. I love how the Passion Translation version of this verse reads:

"17 Now the "Lord" I'm referring to is the Holy Spirit, and wherever He is Lord, there is freedom."

Where is Holy Spirit? John 7:38-39 tells us.

John 7:38-39 (TPT)
"Believe in me (Jesus) so that rivers of living water will burst out from within you, flowing from your innermost being, just like the Scripture says!'" Jesus was prophesying about the Holy Spirit that believers were being prepared to receive. But the Holy Spirit had not yet been poured out upon them, because Jesus had not yet been unveiled in his full splendor."

John 7:38-39 (NKJV)
"38 He who believes in Me (Jesus), as the Scripture said, 'From his innermost being shall flow rivers of living water.' 39 But this He spoke of the Spirit, whom those who believe in Him were to receive; for the Spirit was not yet given, because Jesus was not yet glorified."

If you are a born-again believer in Jesus Christ, then God's very Spirit lives inside of you. Holy Spirit is referred to many times in Scripture as a river. His Spirit flows in you and out of you like a river according to the Word. Isn't that wonderful? To think that Almighty God, Creator of everything, all powerful, all knowing, perfect and Holy God of all chose to come and make His home in His people as they choose to surrender to Him is amazing. The Scripture says, *"wherever He is Lord, there is freedom."* Every area of your life that is surrendered to Holy Spirit will be freed from the bondage and captivity of the evil one because where He is Lord, there is freedom.

The Bible says that we are His temple in 1 Corinthians 6:19. *"19 Or do you not know that your body is the temple of the Holy Spirit who is in you, whom you have from God, and you are not your own?"* This is a very powerful Scripture. Again, God's Spirit is alive within His children. As we surrender to Him, we die to ourselves. This verse says that we are no longer our own! We were bought with a price, the very blood of Jesus, and we are to submit to Holy Spirit's every whisper in our lives. We lay down our plans and our desires to flow with His. It is a beautiful surrender because His plans for us are so much greater than we could ever imagine!

As Jesus was preparing His disciples for His death, He told them about the coming Holy Spirit. Understandably, His disciples were saddened at the news that Jesus was about to leave them. They were probably very scared and wondered what these last three years of following Jesus had been about. No doubt they felt abandoned and confused. It didn't look like they thought it would. Amidst all these emotions, Jesus comforted them with these words from John 14:16-18:

"16 And I will pray the Father, and He will give you another Helper, that He may abide with you forever— 17 the Spirit of truth, whom the world cannot receive, because it neither sees Him nor knows Him; but you know Him, for He dwells with you and will be in you. 18 I wll not leave you orphans; I will come to you."

He speaks of this again in John 16:6-7:

"6 But because I have said these things to you, sorrow has filled your heart. 7 Nevertheless, I tell you the truth. It is to your advantage that I go away; for if I do not go away, the Helper will not come to you; but if I depart, I will send Him to you."

Jesus was letting His disciples know that His very representative would come and that it would be even better for them. How could this be? Because Jesus lived and moved among them. When Holy Spirit came, He would live in them. Just as the Father sent Jesus, Jesus was sending Holy Spirit. Holy Spirit is the full representation of Jesus in the earth today.

I hope you are seeing that Holy Spirit is powerful and very much a part of the Godhead. He was with the Father and Son in the beginning at creation. He has always been and will always be. Father, Son and Holy Spirit are the three in one, each carrying different roles and functions within the Godhead. Different functions, but perfectly united as one. Holy Spirit is a "He"; Holy Spirit is a person just like both God and Jesus are persons and He is to be honored as such. He is a gift to us according to Acts 2:38:

> *"38 Then Peter said to them, 'Repent, and let every one of you be baptized in the name of Jesus Christ for the remission of sins; and you shall receive the gift of the Holy Spirit."*

Titles of Holy Spirit

All throughout the Word of God, Holy Spirit is referred to in many ways. Below are just a few of the titles of Holy Spirit. He is the

- Spirit of Life (Romans 8:2)
- Spirit of Truth (John 16:13; 1 John 4:6)
- Spirit of Glory (1 Peter 4:14)
- Spirit of Grace (Hebrews 1:17)
- Spirit of Wisdom and Revelation (Ephesians 1:17)
- Spirit of Promise (Ephesians 1:3)
- Spirit of Holiness (Romans 1:4)
- Holy Ghost (1 Corinthians 12:3)
- Comforter/Intercessor (John 15:26)
- Spirit of Jesus (1 Peter 1:11)
- Spirit of the Son (Galatians 4:6)
- Spirit of the Living God (2 Corinthians 3:3)
- Spirit of the Father (Matthew 10:20)

The 7-Fold Spirit of God – The Fullness of God's Spirit

Isaiah 11:1-5
*"1 There shall come forth a Rod from the stem of Jesse,
And a Branch shall grow out of his roots.
2 The Spirit of the Lord shall rest upon Him,
The Spirit of wisdom and understanding,*

*The Spirit of counsel and might,
The Spirit of knowledge and of the fear of the Lord.
3 His delight is in the fear of the Lord,
And He shall not judge by the sight of His eyes,
Nor decide by the hearing of His ears;
4 But with righteousness He shall judge the poor,
And decide with equity for the meek of the earth;
He shall strike the earth with the rod of His mouth,
And with the breath of His lips He shall slay the wicked.
5 Righteousness shall be the belt of His loins,
And faithfulness the belt of His waist."*

The seven-fold Spirit of God (Spirit of the Lord, Spirit of Wisdom, Spirit of Understanding, Spirit of Council, Spirit of Might, Spirit of Knowledge, Spirit of the Fear of the Lord) is the fullness of Holy Spirit. These marvelous attributes or functions rested upon Jesus in power and in great demonstration in order to reveal the Father of Glory and His heavenly Kingdom.

Functions of Holy Spirit

The Father, Son, and Holy Spirit are One, yet, they have different roles and functions. Let's look at a few of the functions of Holy Spirit.

- First and foremost, we are born again through Holy Spirit. John 3:3, 5-7 declares, *"3 Jesus answered and said to him, 'Most assuredly, I say to you, unless one is born again, he cannot see the kingdom of God.' 5 Jesus answered, 'Most assuredly, I say to you, unless one is born of water and the Spirit, he cannot enter the kingdom of God. 6 That which is born of the flesh is flesh, and that which is born of the Spirit is spirit. 7 Do not marvel that I said to you, "You must be born again."'*

- He will lead and direct us all throughout our lives. Romans 8:14 says, *"14 For as many as are led by the Spirit of God, these are sons of God."* Holy Spirit is constantly speaking to us and will speak to us in our own language. This means that He will communicate with you in ways that you will understand. He is a very personal God and He wants to encounter you and wants you to encounter Him.

- Matthew 12:28 tells us that Holy Spirit casts out devils. *"28 But if I cast out demons by the Spirit of God, surely the kingdom of God has come upon you."*

- Holy Spirit leads us in our worship of the Lord. He is ever present before the throne of God and knows how we are to minister unto the Lord in ways we don't know.

- Holy Spirit brings comfort, health and strength to us. Acts 9:31 says, *"31 Then the churches throughout all Judea, Galilee, and Samaria had peace and were edified. And walking in the fear of the Lord and in the comfort of the Holy Spirit, they were multiplied."*

- Holy Spirit will show us things to come. *"13 However, when He, the Spirit of truth, has come, He will guide you into all truth; for He will not speak on His own authority, but what-*

ever He hears He will speak; and He will tell you things to come" (John 16:13).

- Holy Spirit produces fruit. There are actual fruits of the Holy Spirit that will exemplify His presence in our lives as they come forth. Galatians 5:22-23 tells us, *"22 But the fruit of the Spirit is love, joy, peace, longsuffering, kindness, goodness, faithfulness, 23 gentleness, self-control. Against such there is no law."*

- He helps us in our weakness. *"23 Likewise, the Spirit also helps in our weaknesses. For we do not know what we should pray for as we ought, but the Spirit Himself makes intercession for us with groanings which cannot be uttered"* (Romans 8:23).

- He always bears witness of the Father. *"32 And we are His witnesses to these things, and so also is the Holy Spirit whom God has given to those who obey Him"* (Acts 5:32).

- He releases power. *"14 Then Jesus returned in the power of the Spirit to Galilee, and news of Him went out through all the surrounding region"* (Luke 4:14).

- He gives power to overcome the human nature and the flesh. *"13 For if you live according to the flesh you will die; but if by the Spirit you put to death the deeds of the body, you will live"* (Romans 8:13).

- He gives power to be Christ's witnesses and to minister in signs, miracles and wonders. *"8 But you shall receive power when the Holy*

Spirit has come upon you; and you shall be witnesses to Me in Jerusalem, and in all Judea and Samaria, and to the end of the earth" (Acts 1:8). *"17 And these signs will follow those who believe: In My name they will cast out demons; they will speak with new tongues; 18 they will take up serpents; and if they drink anything deadly, it will by no means hurt them; they will lay hands on the sick, and they will recover"* (Mark 16:17-18).

Gifts of Holy Spirit

Holy Spirit gives spiritual gifts to empower the believer to be Christ's witnesses in order to demonstrate and advance the Kingdom of Heaven on Earth. The gifts of the Spirit are listed in 1 Corinthians 12:4-11 (NASB) as follows:

"4 Now there are varieties of gifts, but the same Spirit. 5 And there are varieties of ministries, and the same Lord. 6 There are varieties of effects, but the same God who works all things in all persons. 7 But to each one is given the manifestation of the Spirit for the common good. 8 For to one is given the word of wisdom through the Spirit, and to another the word of knowledge according to the same Spirit; 9 to another faith by the same Spirit, and to another gifts of healing by the one Spirit, 10 and to another the effecting of miracles, and to another prophecy, and to another the distinguishing of spirits, to another various kinds of tongues, and to another the interpretation of tongues. 11 But one and the same Spirit works all these things, distributing to each one individually just as He wills."

- **Word of Wisdom** – The word of wisdom will empower the individual with a supernatural ability to APPLY knowledge or wisdom to any situation or need.
- **Word of Knowledge** – The word of knowledge is supernatural knowledge about a situation or individual.
- **Faith** – The gift of faith is a supernatural ability to believe in any circumstance: physically, emotionally, financially, or spiritually.
- **Healings** – The gifts of healings are the abilities to heal and restore spiritually, physically, and emotionally.
- **Working of Miracles** – The gift of miracles releases supernatural answers to prayer instantly in any given situation or need, physically, emotionally, financially, or spiritually.
- **Prophecy** – The gift of prophecy is given in order to speak forth what God is saying. Prophecy will encourage, strengthen, build up and exhort the individual receiving it.
- **Discerning of Spirits** – The discerning of spirits is the supernatural ability to distinguish or KNOW what spirit is at work in an individual or a circumstance - the human spirit, demonic spirit, or Holy Spirit.
- **Different Kinds of Tongues** – The gift of tongues is a supernatural prayer language released and spoken from the believer's own spirit to God. Praying in the spirit strengthens the believer's faith and can give supernatural revelation, wisdom or knowledge in any given situation.

There are so many more functions of Holy Spirit. He always ministers in love and brings fresh revelation from God's heart daily. He washes and purifies us and changes us into the image of Christ. He is actually the One that gives us access to the Father as we pray and seek God's face. He strengthens us as He reveals the love of God deep within our souls.

When the Holy Spirit is not honored as Lord and an equal part of the Godhead, the church (and we as individual believers) are left powerless.

When any of these gifts are hindered in an individual, or in a body of believers, Holy Spirit is quenched. He is shut down and the individual or church remains powerless. 1 Thessalonians 5:19 says very clearly, *"19 Do not quench the Spirit."* Yet, we do this when He is not allowed to move freely in our lives, in our teachings and in our worship. We must never limit Holy Spirit and how He moves in us and amongst us.

Holy Spirit is a person, and He can be grieved. *"30 And do not grieve the Holy Spirit of God, by whom you were sealed for the day of redemption"* (Ephesians 4:30). Isn't that amazing that we mere mortals can actually grieve the heart of God's Spirit?

Holy Spirit grieves when we resist Him. A rebuke came to the people in Acts 7:51, *"51 You stiffnecked and uncircumcised in heart and ears! You always resist the Holy Spirit; as your fathers did, so do you."* Not only can we resist His call to come to Jesus for salvation. We can resist His voice in our daily lives by putting our wants ahead of His will. When we live for the flesh, we aren't living from the Spirit. We are in rebellion. We must not resist His voice or His moving in or upon us.

Holy Spirit is God's very representative to us and without Him we can't operate in the Kingdom. By Jesus' death and resurrection, a way was made for us to come to the Father and be a part of His family; and by Jesus sending Holy Spirit, He made a way for us to move and bring the Kingdom to this earth as ambassadors of Heaven bringing honor and glory to God.

Receiving Holy Spirit

After Jesus was resurrected, He came and revealed Himself to His disciples in a quiet hidden room.

> #### John 20:19-22
> "*19 Then, the same day at evening, being the first day of the week, when the doors were shut where the disciples were assembled, for fear of the Jews, Jesus came and stood in the midst, and said to them, 'Peace be with you.' 20 When He had said this, He showed them His hands and His side. Then the disciples were glad when they saw the Lord. 21 So Jesus said to them again, 'Peace to you! As the Father has sent Me, I also send you.' 22 And when He had said this, He breathed on them, and said to them, 'Receive the Holy Spirit.'"*

Jesus breathed on the disciples and they received the Holy Spirit. This is when the disciples were actually born again and commissioned to go and do the work of their Lord! Later He instructed them to wait for the promise of the Father so they could be filled with power. Although the disciples received the Holy Spirit when their spirits were born again, there was more. There is always more of Holy Spirit we can receive if we ask.

Luke 24:49
"49 Behold, I send the Promise of My Father upon you; but tarry in the city of Jerusalem until you are endued with power from on high."

Of course, the disciples obeyed the Lord's instructions to 'wait and pray' according to Acts 1:8:

"8 But you shall receive power when the Holy Spirit has come upon you; and you shall be witnesses to Me in Jerusalem, and in all Judea and Samaria, and to the end of the earth."

Acts 2 documents the outpouring of His Holy Spirit and power as they were filled to overflowing!

Acts 2:1-4
"1 When the Day of Pentecost had fully come, they were all with one accord in one place. 2 And suddenly there came a sound from heaven, as of a rushing mighty wind, and it filled the whole house where they were sitting. 3 Then there appeared to them divided tongues, as of fire, and one sat upon each of them. 4 And they were all filled with the Holy Spirit and began to speak with other tongues, as the Spirit gave them utterance."

Jesus told His disciples that if they asked the Father for Holy Spirit, He would give Him freely, as a Father gives good gifts to His children. They need only to ask.

Luke 11:11-13
"11 If a son asks for bread from any father

among you, will he give him a stone? Or if he asks for a fish, will he give him a serpent instead of a fish? 12 Or if he asks for an egg, will he offer him a scorpion? 13 If you then, being evil, know how to give good gifts to your children, how much more will your heavenly Father give the Holy Spirit to those who ask Him!"

While Peter was preaching to the gentiles at Cornelius's house, Holy Spirit came upon those receiving the word and they were all baptized in Holy Spirit.

Acts 10:44-45
"*44 While Peter was still speaking these words, the Holy Spirit fell upon all those who heard the word. 45 And those of the circumcision who believed were astonished, as many as came with Peter, because the gift of the Holy Spirit had been poured out on the Gentiles also.*"

The Holy Spirit fell as Peter just released the Word.

The apostles were also commissioned to go and pray for others to receive Holy Spirit through the laying on of hands in prayer.

Acts 8:14-17
"*14 Now when the apostles who were at Jerusalem heard that Samaria had received the word of God, they sent Peter and John to them, 15 who, when they had come down, prayed for them that they might receive the Holy Spirit. 16 For as yet He had fallen upon none of them. They had only been baptized in the name of the Lord Jesus. 17 Then they laid hands on them, and they received the Holy Spirit.*"

When we are born again, Holy Spirit comes to make His home in us and our spirit man becomes perfect because He is perfect. As we journey through this life, we need the baptism of Holy Spirit to move in power to accomplish God's plans for us. We can receive this baptism through the laying on of hands, or by praying and asking that Jesus baptize us in His Holy Spirit. We may be just sitting under the Word being preached and that baptism comes upon us. We can be baptized in Holy Spirit multiple times throughout our lives and should be!

Ephesians 5:18 (KJV)
"18 And do not be drunk with wine, in which is dissipation; but be filled with the Spirit."

Acts 4:29-31
"29 'Now, Lord, look on their threats, and grant to Your servants that with all boldness they may speak Your word, 30 by stretching out Your hand to heal, and that signs and wonders may be done through the name of Your holy Servant Jesus.' 31 And when they had prayed, the place where they were assembled together was shaken; and they were all filled with the Holy Spirit, and they spoke the word of God with boldness."

Who would not want more and more of this precious outpouring giving us the power to be all we are called to be? Holy Spirit perfects us day by day and prepares us for the return of Jesus.

I Thessalonians 5:23-24
"23 Now may the God of peace Himself sancti-

fy you completely; and may your whole spirit, soul, and body be preserved blameless at the coming of our Lord Jesus Christ. 24 He who calls you is faithful, who also will do it."

Love for the Truth

The Father desires for us to KNOW the love He has for us as His children! He has delivered us from sin, hell and the grave through our faith in Christ Jesus, and His finished work on the cross, and His powerful resurrection!

I John 3:1-3
"1 Behold what manner of love the Father has bestowed on us, that we should be called children of God! Therefore, the world does not know us, because it did not know Him. 2 Beloved, now we are children of God; and it has not yet been revealed what we shall be, but we know that when He is revealed, we shall be like Him, for we shall see Him as He is. 3 And everyone who has this hope in Him purifies himself, just as He is pure."

The Father wants us to know and believe the truth of His Word and to actually love the truth!

John 17:7 says, *"Thy word is truth."*

John 8:31-32 says, *"31 Then Jesus said to those Jews who believed Him, 'If you abide in My word, you are My disciples indeed. 32 And you shall know the truth, and the truth shall make you free.'"*

Ephesians 5:8-9 says, *"8 For you were once darkness, but now you are light in the Lord. Walk as children of light, 9 for the fruit of the Spirit is in all goodness, righteousness and truth."*

II Thessalonians 2:13 says, *"13 But we are bound to give thanks to God always for you, brethren beloved by the Lord, because God from the beginning chose you for salvation through sanctification by the Spirit and belief in the truth."*

When the children of God love the truth, Holy Spirt empowers us to obey the truth we believe!

I Peter 1:22-25
"22 Since you have purified your souls in obeying the truth through the Spirit in sincere love of the brethren, love one another fervently with a pure heart, 23 having been born again, not of corruptible seed but incorruptible, through the word of God which lives and abides forever, 24 because 'All flesh is as grass, and all the glory of man as the flower of the grass. The grass withers, and its flower falls away, 25 But the word of the Lord endures forever.' Now this is the word which by the gospel was preached to you."

The Word of God states that lawlessness will increase in the world and the love of the truth will decrease through the power of deception and lies. Therefore, it is imperative that the children of God choose daily to not only believe His Word but to love His Word and cherish His truth in their hearts.

II Thessalonians 2:7-14
"7 For the mystery of lawlessness is already at work; only He who now restrains will do so

until He is taken out of the way. 8 And then the lawless one will be revealed, whom the Lord will consume with the breath of His mouth and destroy with the brightness of His coming. 9 The coming of the lawless one is according to the working of Satan, with all power, signs, and lying wonders, 10 and with all unrighteous deception among those who perish, because <u>they did not receive the love of the truth, that they might be saved</u> [emphasis mine].11 And for this reason God will send them strong delusion, that they should believe the lie, 12 that they all may be condemned who did not believe the truth but had pleasure in unrighteousness.

Stand Fast.

13 But we are bound to give thanks to God always for you, brethren beloved by the Lord, because God from the beginning chose you for salvation through sanctification by the Spirit and belief in the truth, 14 to which He called you by our gospel, for the obtaining of the glory of our Lord Jesus Christ."

Beware of Deception

Jesus warned His disciples of deception. Deception contradicts truth and the enemy, satan, will work to deceive people and twist God's Word in order to lead people astray. When people are deceived, they do not know they are!

Matthew 24:4-5
"4 And Jesus answered and said to them: 'Take heed that no one deceives you. 5 For many will come in My name, saying, "I am the Christ,"

and will deceive many."

Matthew 24:11-12
"11 Then many false prophets will rise up and deceive many. 12 And because lawlessness will abound, the love of many will grow cold."

Matthew 24:24-25
"24 For false christs and false prophets will rise and show great signs and wonders to deceive, if possible, even the elect. 25 See, I have told you beforehand."

Satan comes against the truth of God's Word and He will oppose those who follow Jesus. This is an anti-christ spirit according to I John 2:18-21 that opposed the disciples and will come again before Jesus returns:

I John 2:18-21
"18 Little children, it is the last hour; and as you have heard that the Antichrist is coming, even now many antichrists have come, by which we know that it is the last hour. 19 They went out from us, but they were not of us; for if they had been of us, they would have continued with us; but they went out that they might be made manifest, that none of them were of us. 20 But you have an anointing from the Holy One, and you know all things. 21 I have not written to you because you do not know the truth, but because you know it, and that no lie is of the truth."

Holy Spirit warned us through the apostle John's letter in I John 4 of the spirit of error and the false prophets – those who are not releasing truth from His Spirit.

I John 4:1-6

"1 Beloved, do not believe every spirit, but test the spirits, whether they are of God; because many false prophets have gone out into the world. 2 By this you know the Spirit of God: Every spirit that confesses that Jesus Christ has come in the flesh is of God, 3 and every spirit that does not confess that Jesus Christ has come in the flesh is not of God. And this is the spirit of the Antichrist, which you have heard was coming, and is now already in the world.

4 You are of God, little children, and have overcome them, because He who is in you is greater than he who is in the world. 5 They are of the world. Therefore they speak as of the world, and the world hears them. 6 We are of God. He who knows God hears us; he who is not of God does not hear us. <u>By this we know the spirit of truth and the spirit of error</u> [emphasis mine]."

The apostle Paul warned the church about false apostles, prophets and teachers who would infiltrate the church in order to turn them away from the truth and our Lord's Gospel.

Acts 20:28-30

"28 Be on guard for yourselves and for all the flock, among which the Holy Spirit has made you overseers, to shepherd the church of God which He purchased with His own blood. 29 I know that after my departing savage wolves will come in among you, not sparing the flock; 30 and from among your own selves men will arise, speaking perverse things, to draw away disciples after them."

Galatians 1:6-9
"6 I marvel that you are turning away so soon from Him who called you in the grace of Christ, to a different gospel, 7 which is not another; but there are some who trouble you and want to pervert the gospel of Christ. 8 But even if we, or an angel from heaven, preach any other gospel to you than what we have preached to you, let him be accursed. 9 As we have said before, so now I say again, if anyone preaches any other gospel to you than what you have received, let him be accursed."

II Corinthians 11:2-4
"2 For I am jealous for you with godly jealousy. For I have betrothed you to one husband, that I may present you as a chaste virgin to Christ. 3 But I fear, lest somehow, as the serpent deceived Eve by his craftiness, so your minds may be corrupted from the simplicity that is in Christ. 4 For if he who comes preaches another Jesus whom we have not preached, or if you receive a different spirit which you have not received, or a different gospel which you have not accepted—you may well put up with it!"

II Corinthians 11:13-15
"13 For such are false apostles, deceitful workers, transforming themselves into apostles of Christ. 14 And no wonder! For Satan himself transforms himself into an angel of light. 15 Therefore it is no great thing if his ministers also transform themselves into ministers of righteousness, whose end will be according to their works."

Peter warns the church of false prophets and teachers:

II Peter 2:1-3
"1 But there were also false prophets among the people, even as there will be false teachers among you, who will secretly bring in destructive heresies, even denying the Lord who bought them, and bring on themselves swift destruction. 2 And many will follow their destructive ways, because of whom the way of truth will be blasphemed. 3 By covetousness they will exploit you with deceptive words; for a long time their judgment has not been idle, and their destruction does not slumber."

Jude continues with the warnings in his letter:

Jude 1:3-4
"3 Beloved, while I was very diligent to write to you concerning our common salvation, I found it necessary to write to you exhorting you to contend earnestly for the faith which was once for all delivered to the saints. 4 For certain men have crept in unnoticed, who long ago were marked out for this condemnation, ungodly men, who turn the grace of our God into lewdness and deny the only Lord God and our Lord Jesus Christ."

Jude 1:16-19
"16 These are grumblers, complainers, walking according to their own lusts; and they mouth great swelling words, flattering people to gain advantage. 17 But you, beloved, remember the words which were spoken before by the apostles of our Lord Jesus Christ: 18 how they told

you that there would be mockers in the last time who would walk according to their own ungodly lusts. 19 These are sensual persons, who cause divisions, not having the Spirit."

II John 1:6-11 speaks of deceivers:

"6 This is love, that we walk according to His commandments. This is the commandment, that as you have heard from the beginning, you should walk in it. 7 For many deceivers have gone out into the world who do not confess Jesus Christ as coming in the flesh. This is a deceiver and an antichrist. 8 Look to yourselves, that we do not lose those things we worked for, but that we may receive a full reward. 9 Whoever transgresses and does not abide in the doctrine of Christ does not have God. He who abides in the doctrine of Christ has both the Father and the Son. 10 If anyone comes to you and does not bring this doctrine, do not receive him into your house nor greet him; 11 for he who greets him shares in his evil deeds."

Jesus chose to empower His church through His own giftings in order to build up and protect God's family. He calls people into various offices or positions of leadership to labor with, teach and train those who call upon His name.

Ephesians 4:11-16
"11 And He Himself gave some to be apostles, some prophets, some evangelists, and some pastors and teachers, 12 for the equipping of the saints for the work of ministry, for the edifying of the body of Christ, 13 till we all come to the unity of the faith and of the knowledge

of the Son of God, to a perfect man, to the measure of the stature of the fullness of Christ; 14 that we should no longer be children, tossed to and fro and carried about with every wind of doctrine, by the trickery of men, in the cunning craftiness of deceitful plotting, 15 but, speaking the truth in love, may grow up in all things into Him who is the head—Christ— 16 from whom the whole body, joined and knit together by what every joint supplies, according to the effective working by which every part does its share, causes growth of the body for the edifying of itself in love."

I Peter 5:1-4
"1 The elders who are among you I exhort, I who am a fellow elder and a witness of the sufferings of Christ, and also a partaker of the glory that will be revealed: 2 Shepherd the flock of God which is among you, serving as overseers, not by compulsion but willingly, not for dishonest gain but eagerly; 3 nor as being lords over those entrusted to you, but being examples to the flock; 4 and when the Chief Shepherd appears, you will receive the crown of glory that does not fade away."

God's Word is truth and the Spirit of Truth, Holy Spirit, will teach, comfort, protect, warn, and empower, all saints according to His Word.

II Timothy 3:12-16
"12 Yes, and all who desire to live godly in Christ Jesus will suffer persecution. 13 But evil men and impostors will grow worse and worse, deceiving and being deceived. 14 But you must continue in the things which you have learned

and been assured of, knowing from whom you have learned them, 15 and that from childhood you have known the Holy Scriptures, which are able to make you wise for salvation through faith which is in Christ Jesus. 16 All Scripture is given by inspiration of God, and is profitable for doctrine, for reproof, for correction, for instruction in righteousness."

What We Must Do

We've learned that we are to move in His gifts to minister to people and see His Kingdom revealed. We are also to pray in the Holy Spirit, in tongues. This is one of the gifts that He gives us to use. Jude 1:20 says, *"20 but you, beloved, building yourselves up on your most holy faith, praying in the Holy Spirit."* Praying in tongues is truly Spirit to spirit. It is a pure prayer.

Finally, we are to fellowship with Holy Spirit. This is a constant communion with our best friend each and every day of our lives. It is a communion that is vital for the big things and the small things. It is a great adventure full of such joy and excitement. There is great expectation each morning when we journey with the Spirit. He helps us in the present, and He tells of secrets and mysteries of things to come. He will comfort us in the hard times as He holds us close, and He will laugh with us in the happy times as life brings celebration. He is simply amazing and worth the surrender.

As believers and citizens of the Kingdom of Heaven, we carry the presence of the Holy Spirit in us everywhere we go. He, as a part of the Godhead, is to be honored. We are to fully surrender to Him.

He brings us the vision of the Kingdom. He is a constant companion who never leaves us alone. He has power and wisdom for us to walk in each day. He helps us with every decision. He wants to commune with us 24/7/365. Our spirits never sleep, so He is ministering to us and singing over us each night while we rest. He is such a counselor and comforter.

Therefore, our mandate is the same as it was in Genesis 1:28 when God told Adam and Eve to take dominion and bear much fruit. We are to go and share this good news to all those whom the Lord brings to us. Matthew 28:19 tells us to, *"Go therefore and make disciples of all the nations, baptizing them in the name of the Father and of the Son and of the Holy Spirit."* As we lead people to Jesus, we are to baptize, not only in the name of the Father and the Son, but in the name of the Holy Spirit as well, thus advancing the Kingdom and destroying the works of the evil one.

John 14:12-14
"12 'Most assuredly, I say to you, he who believes in Me, the works that I do he will do also; and greater works than these he will do, because I go to My Father. 13 And whatever you ask in My name, that I will do, that the Father may be glorified in the Son. 14 If you ask anything in My name, I will do it.'"

Conclusion

Jesus desires that the church walks in the fullness of the Holy Spirit, and that His bride (His church) would behold Him in all His glory. He is drawing the bride to encounter Him through deep intimacy, love, and revelation of His heart.

Ephesians 5:23-24
"23 For the husband is head of the wife, as also Christ is head of the church; and He is the Savior of the body. 24 Therefore, just as the church is subject to Christ…"

Ephesians 5:25-27
"25 Husbands, love your wives, just as Christ also loved the church and gave Himself for her, 26 that He might sanctify and cleanse her with the washing of water by the word, 27 that He might present her to Himself a glorious church, not having spot or wrinkle or any such thing, but that she should be holy and without blemish."

Ephesians 5:30-32
"30 For we are members of His body, of His flesh and of His bones. 31 'For this reason a man shall leave his father and mother and be

joined to his wife, and the two shall become one flesh.' 32 This is a great mystery, but I speak concerning Christ and the church."

Revelation 19:6-8
"6 And I heard, as it were, the voice of a great multitude, as the sound of many waters and as the sound of mighty thunderings, saying, 'Alleluia! For the Lord God Omnipotent reigns! 7 Let us be glad and rejoice and give Him glory, for the marriage of the Lamb has come, and His wife has made herself ready.' 8 And to her it was granted to be arrayed in fine linen, clean and bright, for the fine linen is the righteous acts of the saints."

Truly, the Holy Spirit yearns jealously for God's children to have intimate communion with Him and His word. He desires to reveal the Father and the Son, Jesus Christ to all who have called upon His name for salvation.

The Lord is calling His church to holiness, delivering her from self-deception, and the deceitfulness of sin. The Holy Spirit is releasing the spirit of judgment and fire that continues to purify His church to walk as Jesus walked in all humility, and godly character, representing the Father! He is bringing revelation of His manifest glory with great acceleration. The glory of God is being revealed both through the written Word of God, and through His Spirit of Revelation as never before. In this hour we must be a people who are able to discern the times and seasons and know that as God releases more of 'Heaven on Earth', the enemy will mimic the truth with false and lying signs, power, and wonders. The believer must be informed of the dangers and the reality of deception in these last days.

God wants the church to be bold, fearless, radical laid down lovers, who move in heavenly places in Christ, knowing they have full access to His throne, radiating His very nature, and demonstrating His power, through signs, miracles and wonders by the SPIRIT OF TRUTH.

II Corinthians 13:14
Now may *"14 The grace of the Lord Jesus Christ, and the love of God, and the communion of the Holy Spirit be with you all. Amen."*

Prayer for Salvation

If you have not made Jesus Christ your personal Lord and Savior, and you desire this with all your heart, then please, join me in prayer:

"Heavenly Father, I choose to believe with all my heart, Your love for me. I believe that Jesus Christ is Your Son, the Son of God, and that He is God in the flesh. I believe that You sent Him to this earth to save me. Thank You. I believe He died on the cross for my sins and He was dead and buried three days, and then rose again from the dead and that He ascended to Heaven and is now seated at Your right hand and is returning again.

Father, please forgive me for all my sin and iniquity and I choose to forgive others who have sinned against me. I give You all my heart and choose to live with You forever. I believe I have been born again according to Your Word and that I have been transferred out of the kingdom of darkness and into the kingdom of light. I declare I am forgiven and healed! Now, I ask for Holy Spirit to fill me. Jesus, baptize me in Holy Spirit and fullness in order that I may know You intimately and serve You all my days.

Thank You, Lord, for loving me. Amen."

Scriptures:

John 14:6
"6 Jesus said to him, 'I am the way, the truth, and the life. No one comes to the Father except through Me.'"

Romans 10:8-13
"8 But what does it say? 'The word is near you, in your mouth and in your heart' (that is, the word of faith which we preach): 9 that if you confess with your mouth the Lord Jesus and believe in your heart that God has raised Him from the dead, you will be saved. 10 For with the heart one believes unto righteousness, and with the mouth confession is made unto salvation. 11 For the Scripture says, 'Whoever believes on Him will not be put to shame.' 12 For there is no distinction between Jew and Greek, for the same Lord over all is rich to all who call upon Him. 13 For 'whoever calls on the name of the Lord shall be saved.'"

John 3:3-8, 16-18
"3 Jesus answered and said to him, 'Most assuredly, I say to you, unless one is born again, he cannot see the kingdom of God.' 4 Nicodemus said to Him, 'How can a man be born when he is old? Can he enter a second time into his mother's womb and be born?' 5 Jesus answered, 'Most assuredly, I say to you, unless one is born of water and the Spirit, he cannot enter the kingdom of God. 6 That which is born of the flesh is flesh, and that which is born of the Spirit is spirit. 7 Do not marvel that I said

to you, "You must be born again." 8 The wind blows where it wishes, and you hear the sound of it, but cannot tell where it comes from and where it goes. So is everyone who is born of the Spirit.'"

"16 For God so loved the world that He gave His only begotten Son, that whoever believes in Him should not perish but have everlasting life. 17 For God did not send His Son into the world to condemn the world, but that the world through Him might be saved. 18 'He who believes in Him is not condemned; but he who does not believe is condemned already, because he has not believed in the name of the only begotten Son of God.'"

II Corinthians 5:17
"17 Therefore, if anyone is in Christ, he is a new creation; old things have passed away; behold, all things have become new."

I Corinthians 15:3-5
"3 For I delivered to you first of all that which I also received: that Christ died for our sins according to the Scriptures, 4 and that He was buried, and that He rose again the third day according to the Scriptures, 5 and that He was seen by Cephas, then by the twelve."

II Corinthians 5:21
"21 For He made Him who knew no sin to be sin for us, that we might become the righteousness of God in Him."

Colossians 1:13-14
"13 He has delivered us from the power of dark-

ness and conveyed us into the kingdom of the Son of His love, 14 in whom we have redemption through His blood, the forgiveness of sins."

Luke 11:9-13
"9 So I say to you, ask, and it will be given to you; seek, and you will find; knock, and it will be opened to you. 10 For everyone who asks receives, and he who seeks finds, and to him who knocks it will be opened. 11 If a son asks for bread from any father among you, will he give him a stone? Or if he asks for a fish, will he give him a serpent instead of a fish? 12 Or if he asks for an egg, will he offer him a scorpion? 13 If you then, being evil, know how to give good gifts to your children, how much more will your heavenly Father give the Holy Spirit to those who ask Him!"

Acts 1:8
"8 But you shall receive power when the Holy Spirit has come upon you; and you shall be witnesses to Me in Jerusalem, and in all Judea and Samaria, and to the end of the earth."

I Timothy 3:16
"16 And without controversy great is the mystery of godliness:

*God was manifested in the flesh,
Justified in the Spirit,
Seen by angels,
Preached among the Gentiles,
Believed on in the world,
Received up in glory."*

Fresh Infilling of Holy Spirit

Acts 1:8
"8 But you shall receive power when the Holy Spirit has come upon you; and you shall be witnesses to Me in Jerusalem, and in all Judea and Samaria, and to the end of the earth."

If you have been born again and filled with Holy Spirit and you desire MORE and want to encounter the Lord's presence afresh and anew, please join me in prayer:

"Father, in the name of Jesus, I thank You for loving me and I ask according to Ephesians 1:17-19, that You would give me the spirit of wisdom and revelation in the knowledge of Him, Jesus, and the eyes of my understanding would be enlightened; that I may know what is the hope of His calling and what are the riches of the glory of His inheritance in the saints, and what is the exceeding greatness of His power toward us who believe, according to the working of His mighty power towards us who believe, according to the working of His mighty power which He worked in Christ when He raised Him from the dead and seated Him at His right hand in the heavenly places. Amen.

Father, according to Colossians 3:9-12, I ask in Jesus name, that I would be filled with the knowledge of His will in all wisdom and spiritual understanding; that I would walk worthy of the Lord, fully pleasing Him, being fruitful in every good work and increasing in the knowledge of God; strengthened with all might, according to His glorious power. Amen.

I surrender and yield my life to the fullness of Holy Spirit; His power and anointing; the spirit of wisdom and revelation; counsel and might; the spirit of the fear of the Lord and knowledge according to Isaiah 11:2, in Jesus' name. Amen."

The Garden Training Center, Inc.
The Apostolic School of Ministry

The Garden Apostolic Training Center is a place that fosters spiritual growth. The center provides training to equip believers in Jesus Christ for the work of the ministry and to be victorious and free in all areas of their lives through the supernatural empowerment of the Holy Spirit. For more information check out **thegardenstc.org**.

The Garden Gathering Church

The purpose of The Garden Gathering Church is to encourage believers in Jesus Christ: to fully embrace the love of God; to walk in freedom; to carry His presence and glory; and to be equipped and trained for the work of the ministry through worship, teachings, and impartation.

> *"It's all about Love. When you see His eyes of Love for you, nothing else matters. That's it. That's all you need to know."*
>
> *-Brandy Helton*

www.ingramcontent.com/pod-product-compliance
Lightning Source LLC
Chambersburg PA
CBHW021132080526
44587CB00012B/1245